NO ORDINARY BRAND

A MOTHER'S GUIDE TO LAUNCHING FIVE-STAR CHILDREN

Karen P. Jewette, Ed. D.

No Ordinary Brand

A Mother's Guide to Launching Five-Star Children

Copyright© 2019 Dr. Karen Jewette

All rights reserved. This book is protected under the copyright laws of the United States of America. This book may not be copied or reprinted for commercial gain or profit. The use of short quotations or occasional page copying for personal or group study is permitted and encouraged. Permission will be granted upon request. All emphases within quotations are the author's addition.

 June 2016

Published by Final Step Publishing

P.O. Box 1447

Suffolk, VA 23439

www.finalsteppublishing.com

For Worldwide Distribution

Printed in USA.

ISBN: 978-1-7337462-5-0

Library of Congress Control Number Applied For

NO ORDINARY BRAND

A MOTHER'S GUIDE TO LAUNCHING FIVE-STAR CHILDREN

Karen P. Jewette, Ed. D.

Dedication

For my husband, who trusted me and walked alongside me in branding our children. You are such a wonderful father, and I appreciate and love you for the sacrifices you have made to ensure that our children are successful.

For our five marvelous and spectacular children: Kiara, Kayla, Krysta, Gregory and Kamarie who amaze me each and every day with their words and actions that demonstrate that they carry:

THE JEWETTE BRAND

Acknowledgements

Thank you to those who encouraged me to write this book. You saw something that needed to be shared when I didn't believe it did. I appreciate you for holding me accountable until this book was complete.

Dr. Coker-Bell, my mentor and friend, I truly appreciate your honesty and steadfastness in this project.

Final Step Publishing, you are the answer to prayers prayed. Your professionalism and patience have been immeasurable.

TABLE OF CONTENTS

Dedication V
Acknowledgements VII
Introduction 1
Meet Our **Brand** 5

BRANDING
Your Children to Wait 7

BRANDING
Your Children to Be Assertive 11

BRANDING
Your Children with Individuality 13

BRANDING
Your Children with Character & Morals 19

BRANDING
Your Children with Spirituality 23

BRANDING
Your Children to Serve 25

BRANDING
Your Children with Knowledge 27

BRANDING
Your Children with Love 29

BRANDING
Your Children with Financial Sense 33

BRANDING
Your Children How to Fail 35

BRANDING
Your Children with Responsibility 39

BRANDING
Your Children to Forgive 41

BRANDING
Your Children to Appreciate Family & Friends 43

BRANDING
your children to work 47

BRANDING
Your Children to Participate in Activities 51

BRANDING
Your Children to Protect and Take Care of Each Other 53

Conclusion 57
Appendices 59

Introduction

SHAKESPEARE ASKED, "What is in a name?" Well, a name carries many connotations, but it mostly carries our brand or who we are. One's name can carry negative or positive images.

After church one Sunday, a member came up to me and said, "I just saw your brand on the pulpit." I was confused at first, but then I realized that she was talking about three of my five children. By her smile and relaxed demeanor, I knew that it was a positive light in which she saw them. This made me sigh in relief; I realize that everyone cannot relate to this, but sometimes you just never know what a person is going to tell you about your children. Being the mother of five children has its challenges; I can definitely say that I am not an expert in parenting.

Numerous people ask me what we did to get all five children to be successful? Although I believe that, as parents, we do the best we can for our children, maybe there are some things that my husband and I did that helped to create children whom others consider to be "good kids." Secretly, inside, I knew God was telling me to write this book. I would dismiss it. The more I would dismiss it, the more God would send people who would inquire about our formula for raising children.

Still, I questioned whether I was the person God wanted to write this book. Then two definitive incidents happened within one week of each other. The first was the incident with our church member who said to me: "I see your brand on the pulpit." I looked at the pulpit. Three of the five children were standing there talking to some members of the church. Just the mere fact that she spoke the words "see your brand" floored me—I get it God! You are speaking to me. The other incident happened the next day, when a co-worker came to me and asked if I had a video on branding—ok, God, you don't have to keep hammering the point.

It has taken me a while to write this book. When I would go through adversity with our children, I would think who am I to tell others how to rear their children? When my children would behave or make decisions that went against what they had been taught, several times I have wanted to give up, surrender, and throw in the towel. But, then I would receive encouragement from the most unlikely people and at the times when God knew I needed encouraging the most.

For example, my financial advisor, whom I hadn't heard from in a while and is in her 80's, called and wanted to schedule an appointment, but more than that she wanted to know how the children were doing. Towards the end of catching her up about the children, she told me: "I have always admired you in how you were raising your children, and I am proud of you." When instances like those would occur, I knew God had a plan for this book, even when I didn't.

Again, neither the children, nor I are perfect by any means, and as I type this, I still question my parenting techniques. My children still push me to the limit. They make me say, "Who am I to give parenting advice to anyone?" But the more that people came to me, the more I had to seriously consider writing what I knew about rearing children. I was told that I need to share my formula for raising my five children. My husband and I are often told that our children are caring, intelligent, nice, funny, and pleasant to be around. And we would always reply that God has blessed us. However, the more I thought about it, the more I realized that there are intentional strategies that we used to rear our children.

As we reared our children, I didn't realize that we were creating a or establishing a brand, but I know now that this is exactly what we have done and thus the title "Branding Your Children" came to me. Now, I don't mean to literally put a hot iron to your children. The title Branding Your Children resonated with me because that is what I believe that parents need to do—Put their mark on their children so that everyone knows who their children belong to.

Branding is not a new concept—it was done in slavery. It was done to cattle. It was and is done today in marketing so that it is evident that whatever bears the brand belongs to someone. Putting your mark on your children is not to be inhumane or as a marketing ploy, we chose to brand our children

Introduction

so that they will be productive, constructive, competent, kind, and caring members of society.

You see, a brand is who we are. It creates a personality and a unique product. Brands serve to bring things to life and change how we view the world. So, I suppose that with our children, we have been branding them with that purpose—to change the world and how people view it through them. Again, I don't mean to literally put a hot iron to our children as cattlemen did with their livestock. I do mean that a mark, logo, or symbol should be permanently imprinted on your children so that they know who they are and if they are lost or wander off, others know to whom they belong and will return them to you.

So when the church member told me she saw our brand, I thought more about it, and she was telling me that she saw the markings or characteristics on our children that we had branded upon them that exemplified that they belonged to us.

Another meaning that came to mind in regards to branding refers to companies, organizations, or merchandise. The purpose of branding in companies, organizations, or merchandise is for identification, ownership, quality, and differentiation. When I really pondered the branding of our children, I decided that these aforementioned attributes, along with empowering them, educating them, enlightening them, and encouraging them, are crucial in their rearing. We wanted, and still desire for (just because they are adults doesn't mean the branding discontinues), our children to know that their brand gives them a sense of belonging, aspiration, a strong heritage, leadership skills, quality, and prestige.

Through this book, I hope that you will consider and think about the brand you are creating, will create, or have created for your children. I still consider and seek out how to improve our brand for our children so that our influence and legacy will continue onto the next generation to be branded.

Exactly who are these children that we have been branding for the past 29 years?

Meet Our Brand

KIARA: Our first born, loves soccer and volunteering, avid reader, compassionate about ensuring that public policy helps all children receive a quality education.

KAYLA: Our second born, loves dancing, straight-forward, compassionate about using dance therapy to help children and adults overcome obstacles.

KRYSTA: Our third born, twin to Gregory, nurturing, creative, loves music, compassionate about teaching and counseling to empower others.

GREGORY II: Our fourth born, twin to Krysta, family-oriented, athletic, loves to cook, compassionate about being an entrepreneur to help strengthen others.

KAMARIE: Our fifth born, believes soccer is life, athletic, no-nonsense, compassionate about using math and science as a civil engineer to safely improve our roadways.

In the following chapters you will learn the branding strategies that were used to help them become children of character, kindness, courage, and compassion.

BRANDING
Your Children to Wait

We must let go of the life we have planned, so as to accept the one that is waiting for us.
—Joseph Campbell

WAITING IS HARD for any person, but getting a child to understand the concept of waiting is even harder. Trying to get my children to wait required a great deal of patience. Whether it was teaching them to wait their turn in line, to wait for dessert after dinner, to wait for their turn to get into the game, or to wait for church to be over since a lot of explaining was needed when they were young. Waiting is just hard. However, probably the hardest part of waiting when you have five children is for them to wait their turn for something, especially when they have seen their older sibling get something they have been wanting.

My oldest, Kiara, didn't get a cell phone until she was 16 years old. I remember on her 16th birthday we had her phone all wrapped up. My husband dialed her number. The package rang. I can still see her younger sister, Kayla, jumping up and down, screaming because she knew what was happening. Her words were, "I can't wait until I get mine!" For everything there is a time and season, is one of the lessons we had to teach our children. Just because you are a certain age doesn't mean you are entitled to receive something. You have to prove that you are capable and responsible enough to take care of it.

Kayla's phone came before her 16th birthday because she was just that responsible, capable, and it was a necessity, due to her involvement in numerous activities. The younger children, Krysta, Gregory, and Kamarie had made up in their minds that their wait wouldn't be as long to get their phones because Kayla had gotten her phone earlier than Kiara. Again, we had to help them understand that they still had to wait and when the time was right they would receive their phones. As children mature and get older, you would think that the waiting would be easier. Honestly it is harder. They are so used to getting things quickly (food from the microwave, information from the internet, etc.,) that waiting requires a great deal of patience: something that has to be learned.

Sometimes, as the parent, I still have a difficult time waiting for my children, not literally waiting for them to appear, as when the twins were born. Krysta made her appearance quick and easy. Gregory made us wait an entire hour before he decided to make his entrance. No, I'm not talking about that kind of wait, but waiting on what God has for them. As a parent, you want to see them do well and go far. Waiting on and trusting in God to materialize what it is they are to have is a waiting game. Teaching the children to wait on God, because He knows the plans that He has for them, sometimes sounded like spiritual jargon, but when they actually saw it manifested, they increased their faith.

For example, when Kayla was applying to colleges it was hard for her to wait to hear the decision that God had made for her. She didn't like the decision. You see, she applied to three colleges. One was in a rural community where she was accepted. She said no. One was in a sprawling metropolitan area. This is where her sister went and the one she really wanted to go to. She was wait-listed.

Let me interject here. Being put on a wait list caused a real confrontation between her and God. She couldn't understand why God didn't just let her into the school she wanted. She, as she put it, had been a good girl, went to church, was kind of nice to people, had good grades, participated in activities, did community service work—and she was wait-listed! How dare God! To make matters worse, her best friend had been accepted. That took a lot of conversations about God's purpose for her and God's plan for her life. She wasn't convinced.

The final school that she had applied to was forty minutes from home. It was too close in her eyes. She thought we would be popping in unannounced. When we visited the school so that she could actually see the campus, her comment was: "I didn't want to like it, but I do."

She was still waiting to hear from her number one school and time was drawing near to make a decision. She could have waited on the school she wanted, but she decided that the closer school would be her choice. Her school of choice, she soon discovered, was the BEST choice. At her college, she started a new organization. She was able to travel and perform with her professor, and she was writing her own journey.

Getting the children to wait their turn is hard, especially when they see their siblings doing well.

Invariably, their question is: When will it be my turn?

My response is always: God knows when it is your turn because God creates the opportunity and the time for you. When God says that you are ready, then your turn will come.

The children are still learning that, and so am I. To be honest, you want to see your children do well and be successful, but I have learned that it is still in God's timing. God created them, knows what they can handle, and when they can handle it. So, I would talk to God and say, "Lord you created them, you knew them before they were in my womb, you know the plans you have for them."

Even more important when teaching our children how to wait is that we must teach our children to wait with a good attitude. Nothing is worse than to wait with our lips poked out and pouting. I remember telling them that having a bad attitude while waiting is not going to make the wait less, if anything it may lengthen the time.

PRAYER: *Lord, please help me to follow Your plan and not my plan. Please help me to guide our children towards You in all situations. Lord, help me to wait on You, teach the children the importance of waiting on You, and to wait with a good attitude. Your word tells us to wait upon You and be of good courage and You will strengthen us. (Psalm 27:14) Father, show me how to help Your children, the ones You created to do this. Amen.*

Branding
Your Children to Be Assertive

There is nothing intelligent about not standing up for yourself. You may not win every battle. However, everyone will at least know what you stood for—YOU.
—Shannon L. Alder

TEACHING YOUR CHILDREN to speak up for themselves can come back to bite you in the butt. However, bite marks do heal. Early on, when the children were young, my husband and I—more so my husband—taught the children to use their voices. I remember us being at a fast food restaurant. I would ask the kids what they wanted so I could give the order to the cashier. My husband would say, no let them tell the cashier what they want. They have to learn early how to let people know what they want and how they want it. So I stepped aside, and the children proceeded to give their orders to the cashier.

"No pickles, no mustard, hot french fries, little ice."

I stood there amazed and proud at the same moment. I realized that my husband was right. They needed their voices to be heard and not their mother's. From then on when an opportunity presented itself, I would make sure they had a chance to speak their opinions.

Sometimes I do wish they weren't so assertive. When we would have family meetings, boy would they assert their opinions about how things were done around the house. This transitioned into their classrooms, into their clubs, into church, and into their sport activities.

NO ORDINARY BRAND

Some of the children are more assertive than the others, but they each have no problems expressing themselves about topics and ideas—even if I or their father do not agree.

On one occasion our son, Gregory, stood his ground about not being in a dramatic performance at church. As the mother, I usually pull rank, but not this time. The director of the play asked me if Gregory could portray Jesus in the resurrection play. He was primarily chosen because of his stature and his dreadlocks. Of course I said, "Yes! Our son can play the main character for the Easter performance."

When I told Gregory about his part, he looked at me and said, "Mom, I can't do this part."

I thought maybe he was fearful, but it was much deeper than that. It took a lot of assertiveness to stand up to me, but Gregory did it. He informed me that it was not because of fear that he didn't want the part; he felt that it was too much responsibility for a 16-year-old. He did not want to confuse younger children. He felt that if he portrayed Jesus, people would place him on a pedestal he didn't want to be upon. He didn't want to disappoint people, because, as he said, "I am still a child and I'm going to mess up and make mistakes."

I gained so much more respect for my son. He stood up for his belief, and when he shared his position with the director, she also developed an even greater respect for him. When teaching your children to be assertive, teaching them to be respectful when sticking up for themselves, or someone else, is pivotal in their development. It is, as the saying goes, not what you say, but how you say it.

PRAYER: *Heavenly Father, I ask that you give each of your children the strength to stand for those things that they believe in. I ask that you give them the ability to know when to speak and when to be quiet. Lord, grant them the wisdom to know that you are always fighting for them and that they can depend upon you to win their battles. Amen.*

BRANDING
YOUR CHILDREN WITH INDIVIDUALITY

> *"To be yourself in a world that is constantly trying to make you something else is the greatest accomplishment."*
> *—Ralph Waldo Emerson*

BUSINESSES WANT THEIR customers to return, and they seek ways to differentiate themselves from their competitors. Therefore, each brand has to be unique, different, and unforgettable. As we rear our children and nurture them, one of the best things a parent can do is to notice their aptitudes, skills, interests, likes, dislikes, and passions. We need to help each child determine his or her differences from others, even siblings. Also, not only must they know their differences, but know how to use those differences to pursue their passions and to help our world. It is their distinct differences that create in them their individuality.

Having children with different personalities seems as though it should be a given, but when you have five children, others often seem to think that they should be alike or at least have some personality traits that are similar. What I have learned from raising five children is that, as a parent, I had to accept their differences, and more importantly, I had to nurture and embrace their differences because this was what made each of them unique individuals. I learned soon after the birth of my second daughter, Kayla, that her personality was greatly different than that of her sister, Kiara, who is three years older than her.

NO ORDINARY BRAND

My oldest, Kiara, had placed us in a lull. When she was born, she greeted us with a smile, no crying, and her temperament was calm. We learned that as she grew, she was obedient and desired to please. Whatever you told her to do, she did it. Whenever she stepped out of obedience, she quickly learned the consequences.

One time, we were out to dinner, and the sizzling pan with fajitas came to the table. We told her not to touch the pan because it was hot. I guess the curiosity got the best of her. In an instant, she touched it and quickly found out that it truly was hot. From that experience, she figured out that we had her interests at heart and did not want her hurt. Kiara has a desire to serve and make people happy. Her nature is to ensure that people, especially children, are given the necessary tools to succeed. She wants and believes that the playing field should be level and that ALL children should have the same opportunities regardless of race, creed, or color.

As a child, she always wanted to make sure that everyone was taken care of and that they were in a happy place. Her temperament is one of mildness, calmness, and looking for a win-win outcome. Her interest in public policy definitely fits her because she is concerned about the overall condition of people.

Now, when the second daughter, Kayla, came along three years later, her entrance was the polar opposite of her sister. She came into the world screaming. She has a personality of getting your attention. She is, and has been for the majority of her life, active and vocal. She was the one who was always moving, shaking, and dancing. She takes the world by storm in that she is extremely up front about her thoughts and beliefs. I remember a family gathering when all of the women were in the kitchen and our husbands were in another room watching some type of sports; probably football. Well we were fixing desserts for them and carrying their plates to them.

Kayla asked, "Why are we doing that? Why aren't they preparing desserts for us?"

All of us women, looked at each other in astonishment! Sometimes we have to ask her to tone it down and exercise empathy, but we also had to exercise and embrace her individuality. Kayla does have a heart to help others, but sometimes her desire to help others can be lost in her method of accomplishing the goal. She has been told that her demeanor and her ability to separate herself from the emotional put her in an ideal position of becoming a therapist. She uses dance to express who she is and how she feels. She insists that if others learn how to use this strategy, then they can master their emotions. When she learned that she could marry her two loves (dancing and psychology), it opened up a new world to her.

From early on, we noticed that Krysta was a helper, a social butterfly, a leader, a lover of children, and highly intelligent. Her love for and quest for knowledge has set her apart from her peers on numerous occasions. In a world where children are teased for being a nerd or geek, not once has she "dumbed down" who she is to appease others. At the same time, even though she knows that she is smart, she still has a humbleness as not to overtly make others feel inferior to her.

Of all the careers that she probably would be excellent in, she has chosen to pursue a career in teaching. At first she didn't think teaching was the profession she would pursue, mainly because she didn't want to follow in her mother's footsteps (she wanted to forge her own way), but after being encouraged to take a high school course for students interested in teaching, she was hooked. She knew that her calling was to serve in a capacity to help shape young minds.

Gregory, as the only male out of the bunch is set apart already. His perceptions of how things are and how things should be done, sets him apart even more. He, as he puts it, doesn't like to be put in a box. When he was little, I learned very early that I had to be specific with him or there would always be room for interpretation. Things had to make sense or be logical, and if they didn't there was always a long discussion for him to prove his point or to get you to see it his way. He doesn't believe in stressing over the small stuff. He wants to figure it out himself.

I remember one of his chores was to dump all of the trash cans before trash day. Gregory would go room by room and take the trash can outside to the big dumpster. That meant he was going to 9 separate rooms, up and down stairs to empty trash cans. My husband tried to explain to him that it would be more efficient to gather and empty all of the trash cans upstairs first, then the ones downstairs. In Gregory's mind, he preferred to do it his way, I don't know if it was because he was getting exercise or what, but he insisted upon doing it his way. He told his dad, "The goal is to get the trash out before trash day-does it have to be your way?" We learned that experiential learning is what differentiated him from the others. We had to work with that. Now, there were times that our way, was the way and that was that! However, for the most part, I think that allowing him to experiment with ideas and concepts helped to create a sense of independence and self-confidence in him.

NO ORDINARY BRAND

The last child, Kamarie, has always wanted to stand out and not be like her siblings. All of her siblings learned to speak Spanish. She decided to learn French. No one was able to help her with any of her lessons because everyone knew Spanish. Two of the girls, Kayla and Krysta, played the clarinet, and it would have been nice if Kamarie would have played an already purchased clarinet, but no, she decided she wanted to play the flute, Again, none of her siblings could help her with that instrument. She loved when she had teachers who had not taught her siblings because that meant she could not be compared to them. She liked that she had the opportunity to forge her own identity with the teachers. However, she did have a few teachers who had taught her siblings, and I remember at open houses the teachers would ask her if she was like her siblings. Her response always shocked them: "Definitely not!"

One Sunday, Kamarie was going to be giving the opening prayer, so I went to check on her before service started. Another person in the church came to me and explained to me that she had spoken to Kamarie about praying and that Kamarie had told her: "I am not Krysta." They are respectful children, but they each want their individuality to be respected. Kamarie is a data person, not necessarily a people person. With that in mind, we had to nurture that gift which led to her interest in engineering, where she thrives.

A friend of mine brought to our house a bag of marshmallows that we were going to roast. She was raving about this bag of marshmallows because she purchased them from a healthy food store. Krysta, Kamarie, and I were all sitting at the table looking at a bag of marshmallows that had been purchased from this store and wondered what was in the marshmallows that made them so different that the cost would be three times that of "normal" marshmallows. I was reading the ingredients aloud. The words were out of this world! After reading the ingredients, Krysta commented that she was thinking about how she would break those words down for an elementary child to be able to pronounce them. Kamarie said as she was listening to the ingredients she was picturing the periodic table for the chemical make-up of the ingredients. I saw their individuality first-hand and how their differences contributed to their career interests.

Sometimes parents, and others, seem to think that we know what careers our children should pursue, but we have to make sure we don't infringe our thoughts upon them because we may be coercing them into fields that are not their passions. One of my daughter's friends is a gifted artist and loves teaching children. Her parent insisted that she study biology to become a doctor. She was not happy, but she did it to please her parent. She finally took

Branding Your Children with Individuality

a stand and pursued her passion. As parents, we are to assist our children in discovering and nurturing their individual gifts, talents, and passions so that they can continue to be the great individuals they were designed to be.

Helping children to recognize their differences and how to use them to their advantage and for the benefit of others seemed to help them with their self-confidence and their pursuits. Whether recognizing your child's physical, academic, social, spiritual, or emotional differences, as parents our job is to help them develop into productive people who can help improve our society. Whether we like or dislike some of our children's individual traits, we are to help them use those traits to be better.

PRAYER: *God, thank you for the differences that you have placed in each and every one of your children. Father, please help them to see that you created them different for a reason. Their differences help to create this world that you created and in each one of them. You specifically designed their characteristics to be an asset for their purposes and Yours. Please help them never to think less of who they are or of the gifts and talents that you, alone, gave them. Father, allow them to see that their individuality is so that others can be strengthened. Amen*

Branding Your Children with Character & Morals

> *Character is like a tree and reputation like a shadow. The shadow is what we think of it; the tree is the real thing.*
> *—Abraham Lincoln*

It has been said that character is doing what is right when no one is watching. Character is who you really are and what you believe, especially in regards to ethics. If one's belief system is flawed then one's character is flawed; however, based upon teachings and experiences, our character can be changed and corrected, if it is flawed. The root of character building and developing a moral compass involves trustworthiness, respect, responsibility, fairness, caring, and citizenship.

One of the foundational aspects regarding building the character and developing the moral compass of our children dealt with teaching them to tell the truth. Teaching truth can be a funny thing because truth can cause pain, but it can also be liberating. Often we skirt around telling the truth to people because we don't want to hurt someone's feelings or we want them to like us. As parents, we have tried to always tell our children the truth. Sometimes we had to delay the truth because they weren't ready to handle it, but for the most part we told them the truth. Don't get me wrong, we were not out to crush their spirits, but we wanted to help them grow through truth.

NO ORDINARY BRAND

For example, when Krysta began to sing in the choir, the choir director saw how much she loved to sing and thought she should sing a solo. At the time, her voice was not ready for a solo, so I told her that right then, her gift definitely was in ministering through dance and to wait a while for singing a solo. Many times I have seen children put in situations that they are not ready to handle (singing a solo), and afterwards the congregation will applaud and others will tell them how well they did when in actuality they did not. It is wonderful that they have the courage to stand before people and sing, but if they leave thinking that they knocked it out of the park and then go somewhere else to do the same thing, the reception may not be as warm. Then we have to build them back up, when it could have been avoided by telling the truth in the beginning. Today, Krysta's voice amazes me when she sings because it is developed, and when she sings it is to praise God and not just to sing a solo.

We have been honest with them about Santa Claus, the Easter Bunny, and the Tooth Fairy. Even though we chose to be honest about these characters, we also made sure that they knew it was not their job to tell their friends the truth about Santa, it was the job of those other children's parents. They would often give older family members strange looks when they were asked what Santa was bringing them. They looked as if to say, "Don't you know about Santa?" but they never let on that they knew because they weren't sure if the other preson knew or not. Knowing the truth did not diminish their love for Christmas, Easter, or losing a tooth.

As a matter of fact, the children were excited about Christmas because of the traditions we had incorporated. They didn't have time to worry about what Santa was bringing them because they were more curious about which boxes under the tree belonged to them. Each child has the same amount of boxes under the tree, but they are wrapped in five different patterns, but no names are on them. They would guess and wonder which pile was theirs. On Christmas Day, they would see who was correct.

Through telling them the truth, they tell the truth, even when I don't want to hear it. They expect others to be truthful with them. When each family member asks each other's opinion of something, we will ask, "Do you really want to hear the truth?" Each of us has to decide if we are really ready to hear the truth. When one of the children knows that another is lying about something, they will make it known that it is not the truth and coerce the person to tell the truth. Children will lie about the smallest issues.

Branding Your Children with Character & Morals

One time, for whatever reason, Gregory lied about a pair of tennis shoes that he had. I noticed them and didn't remember buying them. He really made me believe that I just forgot what they looked like. I probably didn't ask the right questions of him because of the way he processes his information. Well, Kayla knew he was lying and insisted that he was not telling the truth. However, I was not convinced by her, so I just dropped it altogether.

Probably a month or two later, Kayla and her friend were talking and discovered that Gregory had traded shoes. Kayla couldn't wait to reveal what she had learned. Maybe she wanted to get her brother in trouble. She knew the truth. Gregory had created an elaborate lie. Needless to say, when the truth was discovered, as it usually is, there was a debt to pay. I let Gregory know that I was terribly disappointed in him for lying to me. I would also now question his honesty and integrity. Not only that, he had just received numerous birthday gifts. They were taken away because of his dishonesty. I don't know what hurt him worse, knowing that he could not be trusted or losing his gifts. From that day forward, I did not have to worry about Gregory being honest and straightforward.

Each of the children has had his or her own experience with not telling the truth: Kayla scratched my van with her nails because she couldn't go to her aunt's house to play, Kiara tapped another car when she was driving, Krysta not completing an assigned task, and Kamarie hid papers from school. In each situation, we stressed what happens when deceit or lying occurs, your reputation is questioned and your integrity is marred. We have instilled in them that if you are known for lying, it becomes a part of your character and who you are. From these incidences and others, they have for the most part, kept to being honest, sometimes brutally honest, but it has helped them to become children of good character.

Now, when their characters are questioned they are devastated, for example when Krysta being accused of cheating or helping another student on a keyboard test. Krysta experienced first-hand her integrity being questioned, and it disrupted her world. When one's character is in question, one will do what is necessary to restore it. Krysta spoke with the teacher and offered to re-test immediately right then and there. The teacher saw that this incident was serious to Krysta. She did not make her re-test and even mentioned that because she was a good student she believed her. Not only was Krysta assertive in restoring her good name, she learned that a good name carries a lot of weight and is worth everything.

NO ORDINARY BRAND

PRAYER: *Lord, thank You for the uniqueness that you have given each of your children. Father please help us to embrace their individuality and to assist them in using their differences to help others and to help our world. Lord, I ask that when they feel inferior to others, You will show them that they do not have to compete with others, that all they have to do is remember that You created them and You decided what they needed to accomplish their purpose. Lord, I ask that You continue to show them how You desire their character and morals to reflect You in everything that they do. Amen*

Branding
Your Children with Spirituality

Thy word have I hid in my heart that
I may not sin against thee.
—Psalm 119:11

I THINK AND PONDER regarding how our children accepted and grew in their faith and spirituality. If I had to really consider what made them develop faith and have a relationship with God, I believe it was because it began before they were born. We, as their parents, were rooted and grounded in Christianity; we passed it along to them. While in the womb, they were hearing hymns, scriptures, and sermons. When they were born, there was intentional teaching about who God is and what God can mean for their lives. They watched Bible stories on television, they listened to CD's with songs about bible stories, and they attended children's church. Afterwards, we would discuss what they learned. Before going to school we would pray together, before eating a meal we would bless the food, before going to bed we would pray with them.

Giving our children a biblical foundation was important, but what was more important was helping them to develop their own relationships with God. I have my own relationship with God. Their dad has his. They had to develop and cultivate their own. More importantly, they had to know that their relationships did not have to look like ours. Yes, they knew scriptures and they knew Bible stories, but until they could apply those scriptures to their lives, there was still a void. They had to have their own personal relationships. Also, they had to have seen those relationships lived out by others to even know that they too could have them.

I recognized that, individually, they were developing their own spiritual relationships by their actions. Watching Kamarie raise her hands in praise and worship without being prompted by me or the worship leader, was invigorating. Having Krysta ask if we could pray together for a friend who was experiencing turmoil was refreshing. Hearing Gregory quote and apply scriptures to situations that his siblings and friends were experiencing was mind blowing. Seeing Kiara share devotionals with people on social media was encouraging. Observing Kayla grapple with interpretation of scriptures was enlightening. Each child has his or her own special spiritual relationship. They have to be free to express those relationships in ways in which they are comfortable. Giving a foundation is essential so that when storms come and adversity hits, they have a firm foundation on which to stand.

PRAYER: *Father, I ask that You show Yourself mighty and strong to our children. Thank You for Your presence in their lives. My prayer is that they continue to develop their relationships with You and lean on You and Your word to help them through life. I also pray that they will use what they know about You to help others. Amen*

BRANDING
YOUR CHILDREN TO SERVE

*The best way to find yourself is to lose
yourself in the service of others.*
—Mahatma Gandhi

GIVING TO OTHERS can be one of the most exhilarating feelings one can experience. Teaching our children to give to our community, in which we live, began as early as they could walk. One of the instances in which they were taught to give came in the form of presenting their offerings at church. They wanted to put their offering in the basket or on the table like the "big people." At first, they didn't know why we were doing it, but when they learned that the offering they gave helped others in the community, they wanted to give even more. They wanted their own envelopes to put their money in, again, like the "big people."

Not only did they learn to give in that way, but there were many times that my cabinets were emptied because they wanted to give for Thanksgiving or Christmas baskets. How could I tell them that I was planning to cook that bag of rice for dinner when there were people who didn't have anything to eat? I couldn't. There were times we would go to the grocery store and they would select items to buy to take to school for the canned food drives.

Another one of their greatest joys was picking a name from the angel tree to buy clothing for children whose parent or parents were incarcerated and who would probably not receive gifts. Their biggest dilemma was always what age and gender to pick. Gregory always made sure that a boy was selected because he was the only boy in our house and he felt that he needed to represent the males. We usually would pick one girl and one boy, so there would be peace.

They have bought toys to fill stockings, stuffed backpacks, fed the homeless, participated in walks for diseases such as breast cancer, and worked at concession stands for different causes. However, the most memorable events were when we invited children from other countries to stay with us. These times were life-changing for them. When kids from the Children's Choir of Uganda and the children from the Watato Children's Choir stayed with us, it opened their eyes to the culture of others as well as the horrific plight that children in other countries face. They developed strong bonds with these children, because they were children themselves. It helped them to realize how "good" they had it. They never had to worry about losing their parents and living in an orphanage because of wars. They did not have to go without books to read. They always had the chance to go to school. These children were able to share their experiences with our children and what an eye-opening lesson it was for them.

Branding your children to give back teaches them about life on so many levels. They have been branded in this area, I don't have to encourage them to give, in fact, they will now bring causes to me that they feel connected to and which need attention. Nothing gives me greater pride as a parent than to know that my children care for others and want to make a difference in their communities, locally and internationally.

PRAYER: *Lord, thank You for all that You do and have done for our children. Lord, I ask that You continue to give them a servant's heart. Allow them to experience and see the need to reach out to others who are in need. Father, please use their gifts and talents to serve others in the world. Allow them to see that they were placed here on earth to serve and make a difference in the lives of others. Amen*

BRANDING
Your Children with Knowledge

Knowledge is power. Information is liberating. Education is the premise of progress, in every society, in every family.
—Kofi Annan

WE HAVE ALWAYS taught our children that knowledge and education hold the keys to success in life. Therefore, there were activities and assignments intentionally put into place to broaden their knowledge base and enhance their views of the world. Even before the children were born, I would read to them while I was pregnant. I believed that they could hear me. Now, whether or not that is true, I feel that I was instilling and pouring into them knowledge even before coming into the world. Maybe this explains their success in school.

Our children, like most children, couldn't wait for summer. However, when I would let them know what my plans were for them during the summer months, I was met with looks that could kill. When they were young, we would go to the library and sign up for reading programs where they would earn prizes for reading a certain amount of books. Well, for me, it wasn't about how many books they could read it was more about what they learned from the books. Books were great, but the children got creative and wanted to use magazines, comic strips, and directions to build something as part of their reading repertoire.

So they had to present weekly oral reports as well as written reports about the books. This gave them an opportunity to get used to speaking in front of others as well as brush up on their writing skills. I was fortunate because I was off with them during the summer, but parents who work can still incorporate these ideas with their children. Taking time with children is one of the most precious gifts you can give as a parent. When they read books about other countries, they had to create flags and find recipes to cook from the country. We ate Mexican food, Chinese food, African food, and many other foods. However, what impressed me the most was the knowledge they gained about other countries. Their math skills increased along with their respect for food that they would have never considered eating, nor I.

Trips to the zoo, the park, and the museums always were incorporated with lessons of what they learned from the visits. If it was not for these trips, Kayla may never have decided that elephants were her favorite animal. Gregory would not have known how fast a gazelle runs. Kiara would not have escaped to another country with her imagination. Kamarie would not have learned that women could be engineers. Krysta would not have used her creativity to invent recipes. To help our children to increase their knowledge base, everything and anything was utilized to make them aware of the world outside of our home.

I have taught students who have never ventured outside of their communities. They were at such a disadvantage in comparison to those who had been exposed to what is in the real world. As parents we owe it to our children to expose them to the great big world out there as best we can. When Kayla thought she wanted to be a lawyer, I arranged for her to shadow a lawyer, to learn exactly what they did. That experience convinced her that she did not want to be a lawyer, and that was pivotal because not only did she learn about the profession but also about who she was and was not. Introducing our children to different areas helps them to learn more. It also helps them to discover who they are. So, take the time to expose your children not just with books, but with real life, too.

PRAYER: *Lord, thank You for the ability to learn. I ask that You show our children that obtaining knowledge is important to their future. I thank You that they are children who desire to learn. I ask that You help them when learning is hard and that everything they learn is because You want them to know something. Give them the courage and strength to push when it is hard. Please help them to understand that their knowledge is not just for them, but it is for others also. Amen*

BRANDING
Your Children with Love

Being deeply loved by someone gives you strength,
while loving someone deeply gives you courage.
—Lao Tzu

KAMARIE ONCE SAID to me, "Mommy, I know that you love me because you don't degrade me or put me down like my friend's mother does."

Love is an action word. Children know when they are loved. Not only is it vital to tell your children that you love them, but it is even more vital to show them your love. My heart aches when we have discussions in class and students tell me they are not sure if their mom loves them because they haven't heard it nor have they seen actions that indicated it.

When our children were young, especially as infants and toddlers, we hugged and kissed them all the time. When they crawled, stood up alone, walked, said their first words, ate by themselves, yes there was a hug and kiss for everything. As they grew older and became teenagers our hugs and kisses became less and less (teenagers don't want you showing too many emotions, especially in front of their friends). So we had to find ways and methods to still let them know we love them. Notes in their lunches, winks when no one was watching, bragging about them to friends and even strangers in front of them. Text messages replaced those hugs.

Now as young adults, they want those hugs and kisses again. Some need it more than others, but that is where knowing your child's personality and individuality helps. What I am trying to say is that as parents we have to demonstrate our feelings towards them. Maslow's Hierarchy of Needs indicates that after we have our physical needs and safety needs met, we need to feel loved and to know that we belong. Before we can reach self-esteem and self-actualization we have to experience love.

Another way to demonstrate love to your child is by simply "being present." "Being present" means to be in the moment with your child. This means putting down the cell phone and turning off the television. "Being present" with your child means to physically and emotionally sit with your child and listen to them. Notice, I said listen, not just hear them because there is a difference. When we listen to our children, we are able to better understand who they are: their fears, their doubts, their goals, their desires, their feelings, and their needs. This is not the time to give advice or to judge, it is the time to listen.

Just by sitting with them and listening to them there is so much gained in your relationship with your child. I have loved our kitchen talks. Not even sitting at the table, just hanging out in the kitchen. These were unscripted events. They just popped up because of a question they had or an experience they saw. I can't count the number of times we have been up way past our bedtime just listening to our children. If we were not in the kitchen, I would listen to them in their bedrooms. What I noticed about being in their bedrooms, after I noticed that they could stand a little cleaning, was that because the children were in their domain they would easily share and talk. To them this is an ultimate demonstration of love because you are listening to them and sacrificing time to be in the moment with them.

Showing our children love, I also discovered, included not judging (this is hard as a parent). Refraining from judging their friends, their clothing selection, their music, or their television shows is extremely hard. However, I discovered that the greatest way to let them know that we love them unconditionally includes being non-judgmental. Note, I didn't say that I agreed with everything, I was just careful in my wording when talking to them (I really had to watch my facial expressions though!). The strange thing is that having this attitude created an atmosphere of openness, and many times it led to bonding with each other.

Attending events was one of our strategies to show how much we love our children. Attending plays, soccer games, basketball games, tennis matches, awards ceremonies, and numerous other activities showed our children that they had priority in our lives. Yes, sacrifice of time and income was important in showing the children that we cared about every aspect of their lives. I learned early from the oldest, Kiara, that if we didn't show up and sometimes even make a spectacle of ourselves at an event they participated in, their feelings were hurt. They felt less cared for (they act like they don't want you to, but they do). Therefore, from experience, we made it our business to be at their events. We had to juggle numerous events at the same time, it wasn't easy, but we put forth the best effort possible.

PRAYER: *Thank You Lord for showing us what the greatest demonstration of love is—Your Son giving up His life. Now, God, I ask that You help our children to show that same type of love not only to family and friends but also to strangers. Lord, let them see that love conquers everything and that when they demonstrate love they are making the world a better place. Amen*

BRANDING
YOUR CHILDREN WITH FINANCIAL SENSE

I believe that through knowledge and discipline,
financial peace is possible for all of us.
—Dave Ramsey

ONE THING THAT I wished I had branded my children better with is handling finances. Don't get me wrong, I taught them about tithing and its importance. Tithing is a principle of giving a portion of your earnings to God. They know that their tithes have to have specific agendas or assignments. For the most part, they are on board and have seen the power associated with tithing, and that God is true to his word.

I also taught them why being in debt was so enslaving. I remember when Kiara was younger, she truly had it in her heart that she would buy her house with cash and that she would not get a loan for her college degree. As time went on, she saw that their dad and I were in debt by buying a house through a loan and perhaps that taught them that being in debt (good debt) was ok or accepted. Don't get me wrong, I do realize what the Bible says owe no man anything but love. Somehow, I believe, I have taught the children to live beyond their income. Some things are worth investing in such as a degree or a home. Some things just aren't! Teaching children to save for vacations, cars, and clothing is a necessity in order to live a financially stress-free life.

What I am saying is that when it comes to the branding of your children with finances, teach them to save. Involve them in financial workshops and how to live within their means. I so wished that I had. In our state of

NO ORDINARY BRAND

Virginia, our students have to complete a financial literacy class to graduate. Even though the class was optional at first, not many students took the class.

I remember after Kayla graduated from high school and she knew very little about handling finances, although she was relatively good at saving and not going beyond her means, she still found stress in some areas. Her statement was someone should have taught us this financial stuff, like how to write checks and balance a checkbook (which is probably obsolete today) when we were in high school. I laughed and said it was there, you just didn't sign up for the class. Not as an excuse, but when you are on an advanced diploma track, it is difficult to schedule such elective classes. That is why in Virginia it is now a mandated course for graduation.

Some of the kids are more financially disciplined than the others, but recently due to hardships and other circumstances they are learning the importance of being debt free and are striving to live that kind of life.

PRAYER: *Father, You give us finances to survive in the world. Lord, teach our children how to use and not misuse those finances. Help them to understand the importance of being debt free, and more importantly, how to use their finances to help those in need. Give them the strength to be disciplined and obedient to Your word about finances and how to leave a legacy for their children. Amen*

Branding
Your Children How to Fail

> *Winning is great, sure, but if you are really going to do something in life, the secret is learning how to lose. Nobody goes undefeated all the time. If you can pick up after a crushing defeat, and go on to win again, you are going to be a champion someday.*
> —Wilma Rudolph

DURING A CONVERSATION with three of the children, we were discussing their thoughts regarding being judgmental and expectations of them. From that conversation, they felt as though they had been charged to be examples for others. Krysta, in particular, felt that if she failed, she would be letting people down. I want to address this notion of perfection and thinking that failing is not an option. No one likes to fail or lose, but children have to learn that failure is a part of life and that teachable moments are a part of failure.

Getting a driver's license is an ultimate goal for teenagers: the open road, not having to be driven to activities, etc. And let's face it, as parents it is freedom for us as well. In the Jewette household, opportunities are afforded to the children when a license is received. But first, let's get the learner's permit.

I recall when three of the children, at different times took their driver's permit test the first time and failed it. They were devastated! You would have thought the world had ended. You see, they were used to passing tests. The thought of not passing didn't occur to them. So many emotions were expressed by them, from feeling dumb to feeling embarrassed because many of their friends had passed the test on their first tries.

Now, as parents we have to help our children learn to fail forward. This was a great teaching time for them. We were able to help them learn about many great people who failed at something the first time. Then, they succeeded because they didn't give up. I had to explain to them, in regards to the driving test, that there were questions on the test that they did not know. I went on to explain to them that I was happy that they didn't pass the test (that didn't go over well). They finally understood when I said, "If you were on the road and didn't know what to do regarding the questions you answered incorrectly, it could be detrimental not only to you, but to others as well." They understood.

If you have a child or children whom I consider to be achievers, you have to walk a fine line with helping them to understand that failing at something is a good thing and it does not make you a failure. Don't be afraid to share your failures with your children. It helps them to see that you are not perfect and that you survived. Experiencing failed events in life, children can develop determination, grit, and perseverance which will help them in the future.

Too many times, as a teacher, I have seen students who are not used to failing. They wanted to end their lives because they did not know how to handle failure. I have also witnessed students going into deep depression because they were not taught that failure is not the end of the world. It is expected as a parent to want our children to be the best and to do their best, but not at the expense of them losing self-confidence or lowering their self-esteem.

Our children not passing the driver's permit test the first time helped them look at driving differently. More importantly, they learned that it was not the end of the world. They passed the second time they took the test. After this experience, they would share their failing driving experience with their friends to help them prepare for their test. This experience enabled them to show empathy towards others when they failed at something. When your child can use their failures as a way to help others, then they truly are on the road to improving our world.

Not receiving an award or scholarship has helped them, more than hurt them. They have been taught and believe that everything isn't for them. That doesn't mean that they shouldn't try or attempt to do something. They understand that there are lessons to be learned from the experiences they encounter. Through failing, they have become better at interviewing, sports, writing, and many other areas in their lives. They also now know how to help others who experience not succeeding at something, this is one of the best outcomes for their failures.

PRAYER: *Father, please help our children when they don't succeed. Show them that Your plan is the best plan. Let them continue to learn from failing that it doesn't mean that they are failures. Please allow them to see that there is a lesson in every experience and that they can grow from it. Amen*

BRANDING
YOUR CHILDREN WITH RESPONSIBILITY

Quote: "The greatest gifts you can give your children are the roots of responsibility and the wings of independence."
—Denis Waitley

BEING RESPONSIBLE MEANS that you will do what has been asked of you. In our house every child had chores. Our belief is that we were given a house and we are all responsible for taking care of it. The children were taught that no chore is greater or less than the others. If the chores aren't completed, we are not being responsible. Now, I don't know any child that loves to do chores. Mine were no different. I can't count the number of times we had to remind Gregory to take out the trash or remind the girls that the dishes needed to be washed. Getting them to understand that they were responsible for their chores and when those chores are not done, it creates a breakdown in the house. What finally helped them to understand the concept of responsibility in the household was when privileges were withheld because of not being responsible.

A part of being responsible means taking ownership of your own actions, your own thoughts, and your own words. Therefore, it is important that we teach our children that they are responsible for what they say and what they do. I cannot stress enough that it is important that we teach our children that their actions and their attitudes are THEIR responsibility. The earlier children learn that they are responsible for themselves; the earlier they become more responsible. Knowing that they have to own up to their actions increases their ability to be responsible on greater levels.

Probably one of my biggest pet peeves is when children blame someone else when they are irresponsible. They say things like: "It was the computer's fault I didn't finish my assignment." "I was late because my alarm didn't go off." "She said something that made me angry, so I hit her."

No, no, no. You have to take ownership and responsibility for what you do or what you don't do. If you didn't complete an assignment, admit it. If you were late, admit it. If you hit someone, admit it.

I am reminded of an incident with my daughter, Kamarie, relating to ownership of actions. Kamarie and her soccer team were taking a group picture, as most teams do. When I saw the picture, I noticed that everybody was smiling, except Kamarie. Kamarie had a scowl on her face. I asked her why she was scowling? She blamed a girl next to her for her action. The girl had said something inappropriate to Kamarie, thus the scowl. We discussed that even though the girl had said something inappropriate, she was still in control and responsible for HER actions.

One of the Bible stories that has helped me to stay true to being responsible, as well as teaching our children about responsibility, is about Adam and Eve. God told Adam and Eve not to eat a certain fruit. Eve ate the forbidden fruit. Adam went along with her and did the same thing; he also ate the forbidden fruit. When God spoke to Adam and asked him what happened. He blamed Eve. God reminded Adam that He put him in charge and not Eve. God held Adam responsible. Adam knew what his responsibility was but failed to be responsible. His lack of responsibility led to destruction for mankind.

So, if God expected his people to be responsible in biblical times, surely, He expects that now. Parents, we have to teach our children to be responsible and not to play the blame game. Children need to learn that their responsibility isn't just about them; their responsible acts are connected to others.

PRAYER: *Father, help our children to understand that "to whom much is given, much is required". You have given each of them responsibilities that they are accountable for. Teach them the value of responsibility and its effects on others when they are responsible. Give them a positive mind about their responsibilities so that their jobs will be done with excellence. Amen*

BRANDING
YOUR CHILDREN TO FORGIVE

Quote: "It's one of the greatest gifts you can give yourself, to forgive. Forgive everybody."
—Maya Angelou

FORGIVENESS IS PROBABLY just as hard to teach as teaching responsibility. Forgiving means that you're no longer holding the other person or persons responsible. You have released them or exonerated them from what they have done to you. This can be really hard for a child because even as adults, we hold grudges. We don't want to talk to the person. We don't want to see the person. I'll even admit there are times that I have not set a good example of forgiveness for my children. They have seen me hold grudges with their dad and this made me really look at myself and ask is this how I want my children to behave? Is this how God would act? I really had to evaluate myself and line up scripturally, so that they could see the proper way, the right way, to forgive.

I will never forget that it took Kayla a long time to forgive her brother, Gregory, for eating a burger she had fixed. After dinner, she had so nicely and meticulously prepared a burger to take with her to work the next day. She put the burger to the side in the refrigerator anticipating her lunch for the next day.

Gregory came home that night and saw the burger sitting in the refrigerator. He ate the burger! Kayla was livid! She was so angry that she ranted and fussed continuously with him. Even though Gregory apologized profusely, she still didn't speak to him all week. Finally, she let it go and accepted his apology.

As adults now, there are times when we are together and the burger situation is brought up. They laugh about it now, but that incident caused a great deal of stress in their relationship at the time. Kayla said that she was able to eventually forgive Gregory because she realized that the situation was over, he had apologized, and she had to forgive because it was the right thing to do.

When I teach the children about forgiveness, I have to go to the Bible and tell them that God forgives and that he expects us to forgive. Their blessings are hindered if they don't forgive. There are many examples, in the Bible, where God talks about the importance of forgiveness. We talk about forgiveness in our family and that it is more for our benefit rather than for the benefit of the other person. Today, Kayla has the ability to forgive easier than anyone I have seen. Maybe that is why she is a therapist and works with people to forgive so that they can have healing and closure.

PRAYER: *Lord, You have taught us that until we forgive, You can't forgive us. So, I ask that You help our children to always forgive. Even though it may be hard, I pray that You press upon them that forgiveness opens the door to peace, love, and joy. Help them to keep doors of communication open so that strife cannot exist or drive division among them. Amen*

Branding Your Children to Appreciate Family & Friends

Cherish your human connections: your relationships with friends and family.
—Joseph Brodsky

IT HAS BEEN said that you can pick your friends but you can't pick your family—you are born into it! One of the most valuable lessons that I think we can teach our children is to appreciate family. Parents, siblings, grandparents, aunts, uncles, and cousins make up a unique portion of who we are and so much can be learned and gained by spending time with family members. The beauty of family is that everyone is different, yet there are similarities. Spending time with family develops bonds that are needed.

Of all of the children, Gregory has the greatest sense of the importance of family. He visits everyone and truly spends time with them. When you are with family you get to share and air your feelings. We have taught our children that every family has "dirty laundry," good times, and challenges. We have instilled in them that it is our job to help wash the laundry clean, to share in the good times, and to help overcome the challenges. We can help through encouragement, by calling them, visiting them, sending letters to them, facetiming them or texting them.

The goal is to encourage our family. Within our family, we want each person to know and feel loved and appreciated. From our own nuclear family to extended families, we believe in celebrating and supporting each other.

I think the children really gained a sense of commitment to spending time with family after a dear relative died. We began to question whether we spent enough time with her? Did we tell her enough that we loved her? Did she feel appreciated? Through this experience, I have seen the children grasp more and more how important family time really is. They enjoy hearing how their grandparents grew up in the "olden days" and listening to old sayings that taught lessons like "root lil pig or die," which meant learn to be independent, and "don't take any wooden nickels" which meant don't let people fool you. These moments are invaluable for our children, so I strongly encourage having your children to connect with family members as long as they are going to add value to them and not create negativity.

My husband was especially vigilant in this area. He did not want any type of negativity around his children. He would not allow them to be around family or friends who were smoking, drinking or using foul language. Sometimes he was accused of acting like his children were better than anyone else; no, that wasn't the case at all. My husband knew that he had been given the responsibility to cover and protect his children, and he took that role seriously. It was evident that our son learned from his father because of a particular letter you will find at the end of this book. (See the letter in the appendices)

Not only is the family important, but we have stressed the importance of having friends. According to Proverbs 18:24, to have friends we have to show ourselves friendly. Each of our children has a core group of friends that means a great deal to them. Although the girls always teased Gregory about not having friends, it was actually Krysta that I was concerned about. Due to her leadership skills and intelligence, it was difficult for her to maintain friends. Once she established a core group, who understood her and accepted her for who she was, they became inseparable.

What I like best about my children's friendships is that they are honest and open with each other. They all want the best for each other. Their friends are like family to them, so that means that there are times of strife. However, just like with family, they learn to work through them by communicating with each other. They celebrate each other's birthdays together. If nothing is planned, our house becomes the place to celebrate. Our children tend to believe that everyone should have celebrations the way we do and because their friends are important to them, they are important to me and we celebrate them.

Branding Your Children to Appreciate Family & Friends

I tend to go overboard with the celebrations though. For example, their doors are decorated when they wake up, the table is set for breakfast with a party theme and color, there is a birthday dinner, and they receive a number of gifts according to their age. Even though they love their friends, sometimes they get a little jealous when I go overboard for their friends too. They really feel some type of way when their friends call me mama. I let them know that there was enough of me to go around.

Just like birthdays, the children became accustomed to having Christmas parties at the house for their friends. There would be five different parties in one day. They would be dressed in Christmas hats and socks, baking cookies, making gingerbread houses, creating ornaments, playing games and singing carols. They were happy to be with their friends sharing and enjoying time together. The greatest compliment is when their friends would tell us that they want to be a Jewette. Friends and family are important to the building of our children, and I am grateful for those who have been in their lives for particular reasons and particular seasons.

PRAYER: *Lord thank You for family and friends. I ask that our children will always stay connected with our loved ones and that they will take the time to show them how much they mean to them. Lord, even as you add more family members and friends to our unit, let them always feel the love our children have for them in word and deed.*

BRANDING
Your Children to Work

The only place success comes before work is in the dictionary.
—Vince Lombardi

To work means to complete tasks or accomplish goals. Working can give one a sense of independence as well as a sense of accomplishment. Some parents may not agree with children working while they are in school, but it has worked for our children. Our children have been working since they were at least seven years old. No, not child labor as most people think of it. Their "jobs" when they were young were their chores and tasks that would teach them independence. They learned to sort laundry, clean their rooms, cook meals, and wash dishes. It is amazing what children can do if you allow them to do it. To them it was a game, but it was teaching them how to survive.

When they reached the age to work outside of the house, they did. Each of them worked and still maintained honor roll or principal's list. From working, they learned to respect my husband's and my incomes. They have learned what is important to purchase and what is not. Kayla wanted to take dance lessons. I refused to pay for it because she gave up gymnastics due to a fear. She created a deal with us that if she paid for half of the dance lessons, we would pay the other half.

Kayla immediately got her first job at a movie theater. She signed up for dance lessons and never missed a class. This was something that she was interested in, and to this day, dance is very much a part of her life, so much so that she minored in dance in college. She even earned her master's degree in dance movement therapy. Had we just forked over the money, she may have quit after the first year like she did in gymnastics. She amusingly still says that we took her dream of going to the Olympics because we stopped paying for lessons.

We have seen the same outcome with Gregory when it came to working. Gregory loves playing the drums, and we purchased a drum set for him (what were we thinking because of course he had to practice). He destroyed the set and thought it was time for us to buy him another one. Not happening! He decided to find a job. His job was cleaning a pool for a friend of the family. He saved his money and bought himself a new drum set. The smile on his face was enormous primarily because he did the work to buy it!

Having a job meant economic freedom for the children. Kiara was so elated when she was hired at a local grocery store. We were returning from her getting her license. She wanted to stop at the grocery store that was about to open. She said, "I'm already dressed so can I go and apply?" She went in and applied and was hired on the spot.

Krysta experienced the same success, only she applied online to a well-known chicken establishment. She interviewed with one person and then another, normally the owner interviews the candidate, but they were so impressed with her they offered her the position. She loves the people with whom she works. She started as crew member and worked her way up to a team leader and a trainer.

Yes, even Kamarie has worked! Her soccer schedule has kept her from getting a traditional part-time job, but she has worked as a tutor getting paid to share her knowledge.

Before getting their traditional jobs where they worked for a business, the children worked in school. I have always told them that school was their job and they could earn money for their grades. A's netted them a certain amount, B's netted another amount, but C's required them to pay me. Needless to say, very few C's came into the house.

The children have had numerous jobs. Through these jobs, they have gained so many skills that are needed in our society. They have learned skills and attributes in cooperation, teamwork, negotiation, kindness, compassion, money handling, customer service, organization, time management, and numerous others. Again, every parent may not agree with children working, but I truly believe that being employed has helped our children become productive and appreciative of what life offers them.

Branding Your Children to Work

PRAYER: *Lord, whatever jobs that our children work, I pray that they give their jobs their best efforts. Help them to recognize that it is a blessing to have a way to earn income and that the people they come in contact with are important. Lord, allow them to use their gifts to help and be a blessing to the companies they serve. Amen!*

BRANDING YOUR CHILDREN TO PARTICIPATE IN ACTIVITIES

Any participation, even it is smallest public function is useful.
—John Stuart Mill

ONE WAY TO get our children to experience more in life was involving them in activities. Participating in activities afforded them the chance to meet other children, build their confidence, develop leadership skills, learn how to make decisions, and just plain ole have fun. Being involved in activities also gave them a leg up on competition when they were seeking scholarships, employment, and college admittance.

As a teacher who instructs students on how to get jobs, it is always sad to me when I teach high school juniors and seniors how to create a resume and they have no activities to write on their resumes. If for no other reason, we as parents should be helping our children plan for their futures by having them participate in activities.

When our children were young, I got to choose the activities in which they participated. We had a plan that they would be involved in sports, band, ministries in the church (receiving information and serving others), and clubs in school. I recall that Kayla couldn't or wouldn't make up her mind which sport she would play in middle school, so I signed her up for volleyball in the fall and soccer in the spring. She was actually very good and gave it her all.

NO ORDINARY BRAND

When her coach asked if she would be returning, she let her know that she wouldn't and the reason she was there was because her mama made her do it.

From that day, I became "My mama made me do it!" The list is long as to the activities in which they participated: dance, gymnastics, soccer, baseball, volleyball, cheerleading, football, golf, basketball, tennis, Brownies, Daisies, CHROME, FBLA, FEA, ARROWS, Save the Seed, Ladies of Virtue & Gentlemen of Valor, culinary arts, youth usher ministry, children's choir, and many, many more. Yes, the list is long, but don't forget I have five children. However, today I notice that parents do not force their children to participate in activities. I have even noticed that as soon as the child gets bored and wants to quit, parents allow them to give up in the middle of the season or abandon the activity. That just didn't happen in my house. Once you were involved, you saw it through until the end of the season or year. I wanted them to know that when you make a commitment it is important to see it through, that you have to give it more than three weeks. I wanted them to understand that others are now depending upon you because of your commitment.

Sometimes as a parent you wonder if you are getting through to your children. At Kayla's college graduation event, donning of the kente, she said to everyone, "If my mama hadn't made me do some of the things that I participated in and did, I wouldn't be the woman I am today." Those words still melt my heart. Not bad for being named "Mama made me do it."

Kiara introduced me once when I had to speak at an event, and I didn't give her anything to say, so she wrote her own introduction about me. (See the appendix) The words of my children have shown me that they were listening to me, and my work had not been in vain.

PRAYER: *Lord, thank you for the opportunities that our children have had to participate in different clubs and activities. As they go forth, I ask that You continue to give them a yearning to participate in other activities that will help them to mature and grow. Allow them to use their gifts and talents to enhance the organizations they join. Allow them to be a light to show others the way. Amen*

Branding
Your Children to Protect and Take Care of Each Other

*We need to pay attention to each other. We are
our brother's keepers, we are our sister's keepers.*
—Trai Byers

ONE OF THE joys that I experience as a parent is watching how the children take care of each other. One thing that my husband has always stressed with the children is that they protect and take care of each other because they are the only sisters and brother that they have. Even though they aggravate each other sometimes, well, a lot of times, they take care of each other through the good and the bad. They can talk about each other, but watch out if someone else talks about them.

In a letter that Krysta wrote to us for her cotillion she said, "Words cannot begin to express my gratitude for all you two have done for my siblings and me… You have always taught me… don't let anyone disrespect the family." I understood that Krysta meant to protect the family from others, but she also meant that they had to work hard to respect what family means by taking care of each other.

Taking care of each other encompasses a whole lot for our children. They advise each other, celebrate each other, and chastise each other. When they chastise each other, it takes the burden off of us. On one occasion, I remember when reports cards came home and Gregory had a "C" on his report card. Before I could ask him, "why the C?" Kiara told him, "Gregory, Jewette's don't make C's!" I didn't have to say one word to him because it meant more coming from his big sister. From that point on, I didn't have to be concerned about their grades because they were being accountable to each other.

In another instance, Krysta had just finished tennis practice and she had on shorts of course, very short shorts and was headed to band practice. Gregory was already at band practice, and when he saw her, he went to her and told her you are not coming into band practice with those short shorts. Ask one of your friends if they have some longer shorts that you can borrow. Now this could have gone horribly wrong, but it didn't. She borrowed some shorts from a friend and that was that. I was so impressed that she respected her brother enough to listen to him. She knew that he had her best interest at heart. Because they police each other, it makes it easy for us when discipline is involved.

Social media is what they know and they definitely partake in it. They have their own sibling group that my husband and I are not and will never be a part of. But because they see each other's post and comments (some by the way I never see—I don't have snapchat) they monitor each other. One time Kiara evidently saw something that Kamarie had posted and immediately contacted her about the inappropriateness of the post and told her to remove it. She did because she knows that her big sister is only trying to protect her. We never knew what it was, but it was comforting to know that because they care for each other they protect each other.

Buying gifts for each other at Christmas and for birthdays is just another way that they show each other that they care. Early on in their childhood years, I would take each child separately to the local dollar store and they would pick out gifts for their siblings based upon what they knew about their likes and dislikes. They would get so excited about choosing the gift and then going home to wrap them. They would hide the gifts in their room until the big day. Starting with the youngest they would present their gifts to their sibling. This started out as an intentional activity to show their appreciation and their love for each other, but to this day, this is still one of their highlights of Christmas and birthdays. However, I don't have to take them to a dollar store for their purchases, they are independent enough to do it on their own.

They know each other pretty well. Whenever they see something, hear about something, or know something that is of their sibling's interest they make sure that they inform them. For example, Kiara had pledged a sorority when in college and really wanted her sister Kayla to pledge also, but Kayla had no interest in pledging. However, she had mentioned to her sister

Branding Your Children to Protect and Take Care of Each Other

that she wished her college had a sorority or organization for dance because THAT would be something that she would be interested in. Well, Kiara, the researcher, researched it and found one. She shared it with Kayla. Kayla initiated a charter on her college campus.

I love that our children support each other in their sports, performances, ideas, and goals. One of the non- negotiables for our family is showing up at events. I believe that a cheering section needs to be present when the children are participating in activities and because there are quite a few of us there is a lot of loud cheering. When they were younger, it was easy to get everybody to the events, but as they have grown older and involved in numerous activities of their own, the task is daunting. They have been branded with protecting each other and taking care of each other, they sacrifice to make sure that they support each other as often as they can. They have a genuine love for each other.

When Kiara left for college there was a void, especially for Kayla. They shared an adjoining bathroom. Each day she would ask Kiara if what she was wearing looked ok, or she would get her opinion on school assignments, or just talk about girl things. Yes, a definite void existed when Kiara left. I remember the first time Kiara returned home for a visit. We were all at a friend's birthday cook-out and when Kiara arrived, she and Kayla screamed and leapt into each other's arms. Someone said to us, how long have they been apart and we said 2 weeks, you would have thought it had been two years. The person then said, "This is the best demonstration of sisterhood I have ever seen."

With the advancement of technology, they are extra-connected and communicate every day. They have their sibling group chat that my husband and I are not privy to. (I'm a little jealous.) Through their sibling chat, I've heard there have been heated discussions, advice given, encouraging words sent, and prayers prayed. They are each other's accountability partners. As a parent that is refreshing!

PRAYER: *Thank You Lord for instilling in our children to be their brother's and sisters' keepers. I ask that that the spirit of looking out and over each other deepens as they grow. Please keep them connected and protected as they are in different parts of the world. Amen*

Conclusion

*Train up a child in a way that he should go and
when he is old, he will not depart from it.*
—Proverbs 22:6

IN THE BEGINNING of this book I mentioned that our children are far from perfect. There have been times they have gotten on my last nerve (over exaggeration, I know). There have been times that their decisions and behavior did not, and still does not, remotely resemble what they have been taught. However, I stand on this verse to train up a child in the way that he should go! I know that seeds have been planted and watered in good soil and, even though weeds and thorns crop up, what has been taught is in the root of them. They have no choice but to produce what they have been taught.

I pray that this book has given you some insights as to how important it is to brand your child, or children, and some areas in which to consider branding. When you create a brand with your children, you are creating a legacy that is far reaching and long lasting. Happy Branding!

Appendices

When you are branding your children, you hope and pray that what you are doing is right for them, right for the society in which we live, but more importantly, for us, that it is also right in the eyes of God. As parents, it is our desire to raise children who will make positive contributions to our world and one day as they get older, they will acknowledge that there were some things that we did "right." I wanted to share some words from our children that have encouraged us that perhaps, just maybe, we did do some things "right" in their eyes.

Introduction by Kiara

June 2014

Good morning Grove. I have the pleasure of introducing the inspirational speaker.

When I think on all of the things that my mother has accomplished, the list is pretty long. She's taught in the public school system for nearly 30 years, she's been an active member of Grove and a youth ministry coordinator for over 10 years, a wife for 29 years to this exact date, and a mother for 25 years. If you know my mom, then you've probably experienced her thoughtfulness, kindness, and passion for serving others. My mom has a knack for creating environments that are welcoming with her own personal touches, as you might see at any household event. She has always sacrificed for her family, friends, students, fellow church members, and so many more. And throughout my life, she's always been there, whether it was as a cheerleader, an advisor, mentor, or simply my friend, but at the foundation of it all, she's a teacher— every moment is teachable & there is always a lesson to be learned.

But, one of the most important lessons I've learned from my mom is to always finish what you start. It doesn't matter how long it may take, just be sure to finish. Not only does my mother finish, but she finishes well, strong, & with grace. Recently, she earned a doctoral degree in education, specifically character education. Despite all of her many responsibilities, obstacles, and moments of doubt, she completed the work that God placed in her, and because of all of these things that have been said, as well as those that have been left unsaid about her, I am proud to present, Dr. Karen Jewette as this morning's inspirational speaker.

Kamarie's Commissioning Ceremony Letter for Ladies of Virtue and Gentlemen of Valor

June 2017

Dear Momma and Dad,

    I don't even know where to begin. You both have gone the extra mile for me in every aspect of my life, and I am forever grateful. You push me to be better and sometimes we don't get along. But I have no clue what I would do without you.

    To my mom, you have always been in my corner, academically and spiritually. I knew I could always turn to you and you would be there to guide me. You were there to constantly remind me that God allows things to happen for a reason, and He wouldn't put more on me than I could bear.

    To my dad, man you are my number one fan when it comes to soccer, always at every game supporting and telling me that I was the best and to go get this money. I know now I deserve the best because that is how you always treated me. I love you both so much, and I know I will be successful because of all the qualities that you have instilled in me. So thank you and I love you both so much. You were my first example of love, and I pray that one day I will be able share what you taught me with others.

Coupons Made by Kamarie

Good for a movie of your choice on me

— You make me want to be better

Good for a full day with me w/o me using my phone (we can go wherever you like)

— When I grow up I want to be like you

Good for one manicure by yours truly

— I love you mom

— You are my inspiration

Expiration date: Never

The Children All Wearing Their Beta Honor Stoles, Honor Gpa Cords, and Medallions After the Last One Graduated High School.

REMARKS FROM THE GIRLS FOR A MOTHER & DAUGHTER TEA WHERE I SPOKE

When I was younger I must admit I used to be confused or annoyed with my mother when it came to church and spirituality. It felt like no one else's parents made them do as much or be as involved. As I got older and continue to grow I am grateful and impressed at the spiritual energy, power and connection my mother has to a higher being. All the things she taught and instilled in me spiritually has allowed me to connect to a higher being in my own way. It's through her initiative I am able to find solace peace and refuge in my life. I pray I can continue in her lessons and be a spiritual force and support to those around me just like her and use it to continue to uplift my clients, community and myself.

Kamarie's
My mother is my number one supporter she is always there to motivate me to do my best. She has so many different responsibilities but somehow she still manages to make me feel like I am a priority and I love her for all she does for everyone including my best friends that she makes feel as if she birthed them herself.

Krysta
My mother is the strongest woman i know in all aspects of the word. Her poise and grace are unmatched- her will to love unwavering. She is my confidant and truly a blessing from God Himself.

Kiara's
My mom is a woman of perseverance and strength - she has always been a role model for me because she finishes what she starts and finishes well. Whether it's a doctorate degree, a book or an event - I've learned from my mom that sometimes it's not about how long it takes to complete a task, it's that you complete it and do it well. I am continuously inspired by her and hope that as I continue to grow as a woman, I will exude perseverance and grace as she does.

Letter From Gregory Before Returning to College

Whelp congrats here it is the moment yall have been waiting for, an **EMPTY NEST**... On behalf of the Jewette 5 I just want to say thanks for all yall have done we are truly blessed to have you all as parents & we can't express enough how great of a job you all did with us. Yall did yall job now its time for us to do ours and **WE WILL**. Yall grown now so make sure yall enjoy yourselves. Here's a little somethin' somethin' for yall my only condition is that this money be spent **TOGETHER**, go catch some movies go out to eat take a trip whatever yall want; enjoy each others company & play nice lol. LOVE YALL SO MUCH! Proverbs 22:6

— Gregory II

Krysta's Commissioning Letter for Ladies of Virtue & Gentlemen of Valor

June 2014

Dear Mommy and Daddy,

Words cannot begin to express my gratitude for all you two have done for my siblings and me. God truly blessed us by allowing us to be raised by such faithful, loving, giving individuals. You have always taught me to keep God first, don't let anyone disrespect the family, and do my absolute best in everything. These lessons have carried me this far and will take me even farther. Mommy, you said God has a special anointing on my life and I shouldn't let anyone dull my light. Thank You, from the crown of my head to the soles of my feet and I will keep my head high and do as Kirk Franklin says "i smile."

Love always and forever,
Krysta.

Gregory's Commissioning Letter for Ladies of Virtue and Gentlemen of Valor

June 2014

Dear Parents

Thank you guys for raising me in a well structured home, always keeping God first. Mom, thank you for staying on top of me with my school work, running me back and forth between different practices and cheering me on for whatever I was participating in. Thanks for praying with me in the morning, showing us to always start our day with the Lord. I am proud of you for finishing what you started and getting your doctorate degree. Pops, thanks for showing me how to treat a woman, how to be respectful and to take care of my responsibilities. Thank you for always keeping me motivated and being behind me with everything I do. I admire your will and determination to provide for your family. appreciate everything you have taught me to equip me on my journey of becoming a man.

Love ya'll

Gregory Jewette II

www.ingramcontent.com/pod-product-compliance
Lightning Source LLC
Chambersburg PA
CBHW071026080526
44587CB00015B/2522